Susan Dworski Nusbaum

OPEN WIDE, THE EYE

"Reading this collection, I arrived to where the poet asks, 'on moonless nights, what guides / A mother's lips to find the fontanel?' And it was at this moment that I realized what power it was—mother/muse/emanating spirit—that received these poems and in turn gave them to us. 'Scalded by the beauty' of the places and times of her life within timeless Time from childhood to widowhood (such beautiful elegies here), Susan Nusbaum, even as she asks 'Where will we turn next to find true love?' has created here the evidential answer itself, musical songs that are able to open wide our eyes."
—William Heyen, author of *Shoah Train*, National Book Award finalist

"*Open Wide, the Eye* is a collection of stunningly original, precise, and exquisite poems. Nusbaum's eye for the telling detail is as sharp as her ear for the music of the language, and these poems track the inner life as carefully and movingly as they track the sensory experience of this world. This is real poetry, speaking as poignantly to the heart as to the intellect."
—Laura Kasischke, author of *The Infinitesimals*

"Susan Nusbaum's generous new book, *Open Wide, the Eye* springs from an artist's impulse to capture the pulsing beauty of the world. Intelligent, empathetic, and widely-traveled, Nusbaum is gifted with a broad yet probing vision and an

ear for precision. Her poetic landscapes (as well as seascapes, skyscapes, and cityscapes) can be literally dazzling. Yet she's also impressive at conjuring sound and physical sensation, especially in poems that focus on music, or on the longing that comes with loss. Elsewhere, in narratives, she deals with human suffering and childhood nostalgia, but it's the best of her painterly, contemplative poems that leave the reader stunned."
—Joan Murray, author of *Swimming for the Ark*

WHAT WE TAKE WITH US

"I respond so much to the moving and finely crafted poems of Susan Dworski Nusbaum's remarkable debut collection, *What We Take With Us*—poems that 'overflow the silence[s]' of a richly lived and keenly perceived life. Whether she is imagining two husbands meeting in heaven, the tremors of Haiti—the ripple effects remind us of our own 'power failure[s]'—or the sadness of unused things, Nusbaum displays a diamond-cutter's wit and an empathetic intelligence. Yet no matter her subject, Nusbaum's work is always about singing 'the sublime music/Mother herself might have performed if she hadn't interrupted/her singing career/to do the ironing.' If, in the end, 'Love triumphs,' it is 'through the ecstasy of [her] music' in 'memory's filtered light.' Of course, the poet herself summons us best when she says: 'Now I serve it to you, my love./Eat.' At a feast as generous and nourishing as this, why wouldn't we?"
—Rick Hilles, author of *Map of the Lost World*

"In *What We Take With Us*, Susan Nusbaum maps our way home, always unflinchingly aware of those problems never solved, the justice never found, and the way loss too often just begets more loss. And yet she never forgets the

grace of our 'glittering strand of flame-bright days,' our time spent contemplating the ordinary and extraordinary, tending gardens or a dying husband in need, listening to music or searching for lions in Botswana. These are wonderful poems that demonstrate a love of craft, especially in their command of syntax and the free verse line, and quietly declare a deeply lived, highly self-aware life. Over and over, the poems draw us into the mystery of blessing and destruction that the paradoxically sufficient and insufficient world offers."
—Robert Cording, author of *Walking with Ruskin*

"If poetry is an act of preservation, Susan Dworski Nusbaum's *What We Take With Us* is exhibit A in its documentation of an American woman's life that is fully lived in its spectrum of passions, from reaching back to its immigrant ancestry— filled with bittersweet and wistful old world resonances—to its external and internal travels, to its courageous and passionate poems of mature love, heartbreak, and transformations. *What we take with us*, it turns out, is orchestral in its multi-vocal tones and tropes. Nusbaum's voice, in the tradition of Alicia Ostriker and Marge Piercy, is expansive and skillful, preserving her sacred people and places, yet compassionate in its empathic reach into often-ignored others. A voice this large is rare indeed. But what I take most with me in my reading of this extraordinary collection is the way in which it embodies a life that is wholly mature and completely realized or, in the posture of her grandson Matthew's fourth grade photo: 'ready to take it all on.'"
—Philip Terman, author of *The Torah Garden*

OPEN WIDE, THE EYE

OPEN WIDE, THE EYE

Poems

Susan Dworski Nusbaum

coffeetownpress

Seattle, WA

coffeetownpress

Coffeetown Press
PO Box 70515
Seattle, WA 98127

For more information go to: www.coffeetownpress.com
www.susandworskinusbaum.com

Cover Image: "…a painted sky," mixed media collage on
Arches, by Terri Katz Kasimov
Cover Design: Sabrina Sun

978-1-60381-987-9 (Trade Paper)
978-1-60381-988-6 (eBook)

Library of Congress Control Number: 2016934324
Printed in the United States of America

For Patty Chadwick, my sister.

❧

I am grateful for the guidance, encouragement and friendship of Patricia Averbach, Ansie Baird, Ann Goldsmith, Phyllis Hatfield, my mentors at the Chautauqua Writers' Center, and, as always, for the inspiration of my children and grandchildren.

Also by the author from Coffeetown Press:

What We Take With Us

Contents

1 ...*light struck*

Aperture	3
Ellipse	5
Lunar Eclipse	7
Jupiter Beach	9
Beachcombers	11
Jeep Ride	13
Fragments	17
Small Spaces	19
Giving Alms, Laos	21
Naming the Trees	23
November Maples	25
Pond With Hungry Koi	27
Les Fauves	29
Monet at the Reflecting Pool	31
Star Music	33
Magnificat	35
December Blue	37
Tocar, Tocar	39

2 ...*blessed in the touching*

Shifter of Shapes	43
In Praise of Skin	45
Total Eclipse	47
Helicopter	49
March Fog	51
Bubble Man	53
Jennie Kissed Me	55
Cell Phone	57
Confession	59
Sarasota Sunrise	61
La Doncella	63
Nine-thirteen 2001: Going Home	65
September 2005	67

3 ...calling out one name

This Old House: A Photograph   71
The Brown Chevy   73
Multitudes   77
Recital   79
Hallowéd Be Thy Name   81
Family Portrait   83
Parental Guidance   85
Ode to Jane   87
Holding On   89
White Satin Shoes   91
Home Destroyed by Fire. Eight
Engines Respond. Family Displaced.   93
Condo Living   97

4 ...where it still resounds

Slip Knots   101
Attraction   103
One Red Leaf   105
Found Objects   107
Envy   109
Souvenir   111
Hair Kiss   113
Omen   115
Making Plans   117
We Never Went to Bear Lake   119
Never-Ending   121
Angkor: Frieze at Bayon Temple   123
Adagio Assai   125
The Girlfriends   127
Earphones   129
You Were My Cup   131
Breath: A Blessing   133

1

…light struck

Aperture

As the slit on the horizon clicks open,
morning pours in to fill the space,

sweeps into the impatient day
swelling it with sunlight diffused

across the broad angles
of red rooftops on Chapin Parkway,

images rising on silvery paper
slowly burning-in at the edges,

every view awash with shiny
particles spilling into corners,

even in dark places,
like the neighbors' littered porch,

or the shadowy shrubbery on Gates Circle,
greening into the foreground.

As the world opens, the air
begins to tremble, hovering

over the man picking a half-eaten burger
from the Dumpster, the woman

crossing to the other side of the street
to avoid his eyes. It clings

to the blurred contours of children's faces,
apparitions immersed in waves

imprinting themselves on waiting
retinas to keep as souvenirs,

each eyewitness account a still life,
until the day flashes its final portrait,

slides behind the shutter
to rest lightly inside the stars.

ص

Ellipse

Pear dangles from a low-hanging branch,
rabbit crouches, longing to stretch by a whisker;

sun dips, burning behind a tree,
luminous ruby strained through oval leaves;

shadow stains the grass in slender ellipse,
draining shade from rabbit's quivering haunches;

raven bends a tender lip of leaf,
eager to swoop, to pierce, to break a stem.

Behold the pear, black and ringed with flame;
rabbit leaping, falling, jaws agape;

Behold the raven, poised on the edge of flight,
shadow captured by the furtive night,

beating its wings in vain against the tree,
yearning for an eye to set it free.

Lunar Eclipse

A full white moon
drips cream over the ocean's surface.
Saturn and Regulus narrow their cats' eyes
to watch the earth's umbra lap at the circle's edge,
devour its cool center, scattering the sun's
expendable blue waves across the Florida sky,
turning the moon blood orange.

We rise from the table, napkins strewn,
Burgundy spilling across the ivory cloth,
race to the balcony to monitor the earth's progress,
even though we've already read about it in the *Times*—
the hour, the color, the duration, assured
of the precise dates of full lunar eclipses
into the next millennium.

Gawking uneasily at the sky,
we lean over the railing in the dark,
overpowered by emptiness, holding our breath
lest the earth stop turning, get stuck midway,
lest its shadow extinguish our night-light forever,
afraid to learn the worst—
that what we earthlings know for certain
might be dead wrong.

Jupiter Beach

When we woke after the storm,
the blanket of wet sand
had been peeled back in anger,
leaving the wooden ladder that once
led to the beach below suspended

above an alien architecture
of castle ramparts smoothed
and glittering, thrones
carved from the parapets
probed by curious terns poking
their needle beaks into crevices

in search of sand crabs,
a landscape marked by tide pools
like giant footprints crowded with snails
and darting fish, and fissured mounds
carpeted with slippery mosses
greening in a flash of sunrise.

How could we have imagined
one night's curl-lipped fury could lift
the tidal mud we thought immovable,
revealing an emerald city swallowed whole,
waking into the abundant light?

Beachcombers

Zig-zagging the sea's edge,
we rummage for treasure,
pristine sand dollars, celadon sea glass,
relishing the satisfying crunch
of shells under our sandals,
the dazzle of the collage, beached
in layers too intricate to grasp:

apricot coquina, transparent as fingernails,
chalk-chambered whelks,
ginger scallops draped with barnacles.
Lazily we toe the mounds where swells
overlap at odd angles, crazy-quilted,
leaving seams of foam on the sand,

as a pelican patrols the shoals,
pouch tucked into his drab chest,
slides his bulk across the shore
to darken the sea's prismed face,
swooping, circling as we watch,
until a glint of silver darts below,

caught in the eddy of its own impulse.
Tick of instinct, click of pure intent—
he dives, piercing the water,
rights himself in the waves,
his head stretched skyward,
sack dripping, throat fluttering,
shaking diamonds from his feathers.

Jeep Ride

The canyon floor dissolves as the sun stretches
our shadows, black on red, against the cliff.
We labor past poppies, *Cup of Gold*, glowing
behind a blur of hummingbirds

to the mesa where lightning has chosen
a solitary pinyon to slice and turn to ash,
leaving fruited juniper and cedar
untouched on either side.

Monster tires lurch across boulders, up steep terrain,
our teeth clenched against the terror of the incline,
the grinding of gears cutting a path through the stillness
over rocks we had seen on our hike this morning,

squinting at black holes in red cliffs,
wanting them to be caves where dynasties
of ancient Anasazi once hid from the heat
and, some say, ate their enemies.

The pockmarks are not caves, we learn,
but nooks where sea after sea deposited
tides in vermilion stripes, flanked
by sandstone columns wind-carved into myths—

Kokopele, Madonna and Child, dancing Krishna—
transient spirits rising from the rocks,
perpetually re-imagined like clouds
shifting against the blue Sedona sky.

Peripheral Vision

goldfinch arcing

                over folded
                wings of spruce

paned sunlight spilled
          across a Persian carpet

russet leaf varicose

            against a skylight

cracked terra-cotta pitcher
          with blood-red lip

a glaze, a flame
      at the far end of the shelf

open piano lid

hair pinned with lilac

            crook of elbow

pulsing fontanel

torn ribbon pinned
            black on black

gravestone littered with
fractured seashells

            ephemeral
          in the looking back

as moths grazing a screen
prayer flags fluttering
     too blurred
        the images

          too sharp
            the angle

hinge
   too bent
   to let the shutter
          open wide, the eye

connect
the fading fragments

Fragments

...to the writer of fragments, each fragment is a whole—
Arthur Sze   "Comet Hyakutake"

If I were better at sight-reading,
     there would be no mistakes,
this Bach fugue would come
     together in a torrent,
black dots coalescing
     into the white light of cadence.
I can almost hear the music
     through the bones of my fingers
as I try to make sense of it, fragments
     splintering across the keyboard
assembling whole in my inner ear
     flawless from memory.

*

In Delaware Park Lake—
a string of wooden rowboats tied together,
each one painted a different color,
bright blue and yellow, scarlet and orange.
They sway in the breeze,
a corps de ballet holding hands,
their rainbow reflection
floating on the sky.

*

17

From each window pane, a different angle—
    the silent house across the street.
From one,
    red roof tiles, sewn in stripes against new snow.
Another,
    two tall chimneys, sentries strong as husbands.
Crouching,
    I see dark lids of shutters, blank doors
    hedges harboring sparrows,
        wind playing on white walks, undisturbed.
            At the top, a single light burns in a dormer.
    Someone is peering through the glass
        at my framed face,
            my eyes looking back.

Small Spaces

In the white moon of an infant's thumbnail
the loops of green carpet under the crib

in the pocket of a lost terry cloth robe
left on a Mykonos beach

in the cracks separating the piano keys
the bell of the oboe, the S of the violin

in the hush between the final cadence
and the applause

in the slit between the sheet and the body
between the blanket and the breathing

in the slot between mainsail and jib
the thrust and flutter, in the vee of the wake

in the depthless footfall on black ice
the gap between deception and the summer sky

in the touch of a bald scalp to a skull
the cling of eyes and arms

in the widening well of a fawn's iris at night
in the turning back and in the finding—

the sweet smell behind the shed
where a pinch of violets squeezes through the fence

Giving Alms, Laos

A needle of light
casts an eye

along the dusty seam
of Luang Prabang,

pricks the misty distance
with a spark,

as two hundred
barefoot monks

wrapped in honey-
apricot and tangerine

spill silently
into the cobbled road

like a ribbon of marigolds
unfurling from a spool

past rows of kneeling
penitents, waiting to fill

the open baskets
with orange frangipani,

orbs of sticky rice
wrapped in leaves,

trusting in the power of gift
to weave for them

a sacred mantle,
golden threads

spun just this morning
by a forgiving sun.

Naming the Trees

On my walk to the botanical gardens,
I admired the overhanging plants along the bay,
one with flat round leaves big as platters, one

with roots like tentacles plumbing salt water,
not remembering their names, but telling myself
names don't matter. How wrong I was. It matters

that the name I read on the placard was "Bodhi,"
recalling how it sheltered the Buddha from the scorching sun,
with wide, overlapping leaves shaped perfectly for protection.

It was the very tree I'd visited fifty years before in Ceylon,
where, shaded by the Bodhi, I began my own search
as a young wife and mother. And it matters

that I can name the salt-spangled "Red Mangrove"
and can marvel at its resilience—its ability
to filter brackish water, regenerate the soil,

its tangles a refuge for crabs and herons.
It was the same variety of tree I'd passed as a new widow,
paddling along a Laotian river in my needle-nosed boat,

riding low like a sleek water animal looking for shelter,
Red Mangrove combing the salty stream with fingers,
teaching me what I needed to know.

November Maples

This morning the maples are disheveled,
frail as old women, hair in disarray,
remnants of last season's stunning finery
lying in tangles at the roots,
rust faded to pink, gold to raw umber.

Now you can see through thinning foliage
snarls of seed pods, abandoned nests,
a criss-cross of limbs pointing like gnarled fingers
to a vee of geese against the white light

or a spill of milkweed on a distant pond,
bones left to rattle in the rain
as a faint pulse taps beneath their bark,
soothes them as they wait for a blanket,
sap clotting under a layer of frost.

The maples know nothing of regret.
They never count their rings or finger old photos,
never pray for one more day.

Pond With Hungry Koi
A Wood Engraving

Strewn across his kitchen table,
tools of varied thickness—
graver for gouging, scorper for straight lines,
tint-tool for parallels, spitstick for stippling.
He strokes the blades with knobby fingers,
digs and presses, gouges, smooths,
sculpts the penciled image
into an end cut of Turkish boxwood.

Wire-rimmed glasses magnify the image
transposed to wood, then grainy paper
rolled through an ancient press—
leaves inked in reverse tones,
paper-white, veined and scored in black,
vines drooping from dense embankments
above the prismed water

where three wide-eyed koi hover
under a stippled leaf's shadow,
poised to find a clear white space
inside the tangled thicket, a dip of limb
to herald an immense presence.
Silver tails swishing, light-struck,
they quiver open-mouthed, ready to leap,
to glimpse the artist's face, his gnarled hand.

Les Fauves

Overnight the muddy fields go wild
with cosmos and Queen Anne's lace.

Roots of curbside maples turn myrtle-blue,
hedges are lilac-ed, yellowed,

streaked with vermillion,
grapes of unruly plum wisteria

drape over lattices.
Purple-pink tree trunks

twist silver in the blinking sun;
horse-chestnuts hold their fiery torches erect

beside lindens, whose tight chartreuse curls
unfurl against an indigo canvas.

Suddenly the landscape shrieks awake,
dazzling as a Derain painting.

"No, no," my mother whispers,
"nothing is as dazzling as the real world."

Monet at the Reflecting Pool
(Inauguration Day, January 20, 2009)

He would have squinted into the distance,
his eyes panning the crowded mall to discover
in the rush of images, sweep of upturned faces,
an array enticing as the watery tints

of floating petals at Giverny, tinges of browns
and pinks, flashes of white-shocked cheekbones,
blue frost forming over the Potomac, exhalations
caught on the pale lips of children.

He would have found hints of Argenteuil
in the muddy green of trampled grassy patches,
the sepia of bare trees budding
even in January, back-lit by a captive sun,

every color under it trembling in the center of the pool,
dabbed and splashed with swags of bunting,
blurry shapes of marble monuments—
shared disgraces, past glories.

His would be an artist's gaze, a blended palette—
lemongrass shimmering to amber,
flutter of cranberry against gooseflesh,
one man's olive palm raised, eyes uplifted.

Star Music

On a summer night by the lake,
you can hear the stars singing,
like crickets humming or waves
pulsing under water, with a little
buzz of electricity arcing
between them and your ears,
making you gasp, so surrounded
are you by the sound as you stare
into the foam of the Milky Way,
pitched clear as air after rain,
the luminous turned audible.

Listen. Their voices follow you
even into the January dusk,
when stars begin to fall, settle
on window lamps and porch lanterns,
chased by headlights down driveways,
over branches laced with radiance
like forgotten Christmas decorations.
Pianissimo, they murmur beneath
dopplering sirens, pedestrian signals
that chirp away the diminishing seconds,
the music constant through the wind-
blown harmonics of a long lake-effect night.

Magnificat

This morning, impenetrable darkness—
radiator clang, hiss of steam,
groan of a snow plow.
Arthritic fingers of elms
scratch against the gutters
outside my kitchen window
as a radio announcer introduces
Bach's *Magnificat*,
Mary's words from Luke,
borrowed from the Hebrew psalms.

"My soul magnifies the Lord," the chorus sings.
"My spirit has found gladness."

On cue, the kitchen window
begins to glow with the world's waking
like an illuminated manuscript,
the slowly turning globe
reflected through frosted glass,
as hubcaps glint silver off icy roadways,
lights of a school bus leave crimson garlands
along its serpentine route,
a tracery of leaves, burnished gold,
tendrils against the sky's parchment.

How magnificent the sound of Mary's rejoicing,
the psalmists' rapture embellished by music,
as if a brown-robed monk in his cloister
has pressed his quill pen and colored ink to paper
to praise the miracle of morning.

December Blue

The timbre shifts
from gutter ping to tile splash,
drops leaking like clockwork
after the first December thaw

from an uncaulked corner
of a glass bathroom built years ago
to soak away disappointment
in a raspberry Jacuzzi under the stars.

Blue days collapse
under a snow-mounded skylight
while carols pa-rum on frozen windshields
and tinsel blinds the eyes.

Some drops bubble in glasses
clinked but left unsipped,
some push chemo through veins
in arms grasping

for the life-ring of another year,
until gasping and dripping,
the January light
lifts each lengthening day

from the icy aquifer
to dry in the sun,
leaving wreaths of residue
on the white tile.

Tocar, Tocar

sings the violin
    bandonéon
        heartbeat cello
tensed bodies confined
    inside a small square
        of worn parquet
to touch
    thigh on thigh
        palm in palm
    hand spanning
        dragonfly waist
heads to snap
    skirt to slap
        leg to lock
            kick to startle
fire smoldering
    behind the eyes
control and synchrony,
    brief appeasement
        bending
            sliding
                submission
an infinite conjugation
    endless tango
he to clasp
    she to surrender
        violin to moan
            flutter the red hibiscus
            envy the watcher
    oh to sing
        to touch again

2

…blessed in the touching

Shifter of Shapes

(fresco by Delacroix, St. Sulpice)

> *The storm, the shifter of shapes, drives on.*
> Rilke: "The Man Watching"

Great gusts from orchestral lungs
roar through the forest bending limbs,
whirling sonorities through trees

as Jacob the dreamer wakes, the glow
of a winged stranger interrupting
his nightly battle with a vengeful brother.

Flinging spear and rumpled blanket
to the forest floor, he throws
full weight against the intruder,

knee to groin, fingers entwined, elbows locked,
shoving a sinewy shoulder into his chest,
swelling the thunderous night with grunts and bellows.

But no wing, no feather stirs. Impassive,
the angel leads Jacob in tight embrace,
glides him smoothly across the moonlit floor,

kneading a thigh, molding a hip,
swaying and dipping to incessant rhythms,
holding fast until dawn.

Silent now, cedar and cypress fold their arms,
as the wrestler limps to join the waiting caravan,
blessed in the touching.

In Praise of Skin

At the concert when you touched my arm
I heard you clearly as if you spoke,
despite the insistence of tympani in the Brahms,
the coughing, rustling of programs.

There's communion here at our leading edge,
where we brush against each other,
form intact, senses defined, surfaces
skimming molecules from the air.

How miraculous, this largest of all organs,
following our hills and downy canyons,
holding body and soul together,
receiving whatever rubs against our borders,
all the while keeping it at bay.

Of course, we invite fluids in and out,
exchange gases, Brahms and Cézanne
enter through small openings
to pluck away at our internal strings,
ignite our neural pathways.

But safe inside this singular outline,
we can part air currents, probe
the universe as it nudges and nuzzles,
feel the pressure of a slap, a push, a pinch,
the thickening-over of wounds,

we can finger a lover's cheek
and yes, stroke an arm.
What's skin for, after all, if not
to separate us from a world overflowing,
offering as consolation—a touch?

Total Eclipse

The new girl Selena bends
to remove the old polish, cuts and massages,
rubs calluses from my soles,
smooths my calves, oils my heels.

She speaks about her almost-ex-husband,
a prison guard, whose shoulders required surgery
and months of recovery, injuries from slamming
convicts against concrete walls.

Her voice, light years away, streams over
my reclining body. Only her crown is visible:
hair extensions, half-inch black strip in her part
where the crimson has begun to grow out.

She looks up briefly, round face darkened
by crescent bruises under both eyes,
and a keloid forming on the curved
scar beneath her cheekbone.

Hovering over the horny outcroppings on my toes,
she fades and dips to clip a ragged cuticle,
disguise the reality of my feet
with Looney-Tunes Red.

In a month, when the white moons rise
she disappears—gone without a word,
perhaps to another salon, another universe.
No one knows. "Unreliable," they say.

Helicopter

I'm in the parking lot behind the condo,
face tilted toward a blue June sky framed
by a fringe of leaves, green as a caterpillar.
This scene must be fiction, I think—
a hand-painted plate or a child's crayon drawing—

when I hear the rotors, then see it, insect-like,
buzzing across the canvas toward Children's Hospital.
Inside its thorax, perhaps a baby from Albion,
blue-lipped and gasping for air, who fell into the deep end
just as her mother turned away, or a farm boy
who followed his dog onto the highway
without noticing the 18-wheeler bearing down,
who won't open his eyes when his father calls his name,

lifted closer to that cerulean than I want to imagine,
a sailboat parting the Caribbean to white sheets
and gauze curtains, a cool drink, a soft hand on a forehead,
and, with any luck, a painting of this June sky
outside the window on the 10th floor.

March Fog

This is not a harbor fog,
not silent, not sedentary.

Buses groan through it,
honking horns,

heavy metal blasts
from car windows,

crows shriek from rooftops
with the joy of concealment.

It rolls cold between bank
and beauty salon,

swirls past the windows
of the internet café,

settles for a moment like a veil
over the dreadlocks of a man

leaning against a garbage can
at the corner of Bidwell,

his Bible and hand
held out for a blessing,

ignored by walkers
who pass without a glance,

secure in the illusion
that they too are invisible.

Bubble Man

There's a jog in the street at Allen and Elmwood,
as if the corner three-story apartment building
with the Laundromat in front rose up
in the wrong place. But there it is
taking up space, blocking the view of City Hall

and the new glass Federal Courthouse,
with only a sliver of sky visible over Lackawanna,
steel-gray these days, or burnished with snow.
If you're stopped at the light,
your eye might wander to the third floor

where a scrap of curtain blows
through an open window, and near the sill
a shiny thing— a bird, perhaps—
hovers, then floats across the parking lot.
A spark, and then another. Look more closely.

You can see a hand holding a ring,
a window fan, a stream of iridescent bubbles
pouring out like a burst of laughter
rising over the roof of the Greek restaurant,
pot-bellied doubles wobbling to catch up.

When the light changes, drive slowly
through the intersection and glance
in the rearview mirror. Chances are,
the hand still waves, and an arc of hilarity
follows you unbidden, all the way into February.

Jennie Kissed Me

We were sixteen or seventeen
when our English teacher cried—
put her big round head on the desk,
bottle-bottom glasses awry on her cheek,
and sobbed, the spasms of her immense chest
knocking the stapler to the floor.

Not one of us knew what to do.
One minute she's reading to us—
where blind Oedipus bids farewell to his children—
the next minute, she's weeping, honking
her apologies, explaining between gasps
that her own daughter had moved away
just that morning.

After too long, Charlie and John
got up to stand next to her,
John, placing his hand on her shoulder,
Charlie, offering to take her to the school nurse.
"I'm all right now," she whispered.

We adored this teacher, Mrs. Jennie Stillman,
who led us through Silas Marner and Holden Caulfield
into Richard III and Esmé,
taught us Eliot and Cummings,
Ogden Nash for fun, and odd-metered
old poems, like "Jenny Kissed Me."
She forced us to recognize ourselves

in the books we read, to feel
Karenina's jealousy, Quasimodo's rejection,
Shylock's humiliation, our teenage lives
magically enlarged by their company.

Maybe that's why Mrs. Stillman's
grieving came as a shock.
That Monday morning, third period,
we who had never felt such loss
learned firsthand
what was in store for us.

Cell Phone

When he gets the call from his father, he's standing alone
in a cloister of snow-covered pines at the edge of a wilderness
lake, his head already dizzy from watching the northern lights
cascade through the Ontario sky, his heart unlocked, his
breath held in amazement. He imagines his brother in a city
across the lake, just home from work, pausing on the front
step for a few puffs, maybe a phone call. A kid in a black
hoodie, baggy pants, saunters down Bedford, approaches,
demands the phone. "Get outta here," his brother says,
turning to go inside. Then, a stab to the wrist, the pain,
severing of nerves, the deadly struggle, the fatal knife in the
chest, blood pooling silently in the cracks of the sidewalk.
Later, in the telling of it, he does not mention colored lights
plunging through the thin Arctic air, only his father's
monotone, the hiss of silence that ricocheted off the
mountain face piercing the membrane of his rapture, the
icy edge of despair slicing the ruptured chamber of his heart.

Confession

I was the woman of heels and pantyhose,
white blouses and scratchy wool suits,
not enough sleep and a throat burning
from french roast gulped too quickly.

I was the conspirator, probing fat transcripts
swollen with carnage, collector of rap sheets,
of sheaves of white pages in binders,
proponent of pleadings and pleasing the court.

I was the pursuer of Tyrone Calhoun,
who raped his girlfriend's 10-month-old baby,
and Emilio Cortez, who slashed Father Healey's
throat for the collection plate; my weapons—
DNA, brain spatters, fingernail scrapings,
the slammers and bullpens, jailing and bailing,

I was eyewitness to addiction and mania,
blankness of eyes, stooping of shoulders,
to the wounded, the trapped, ashamed
of their weakness, stained and discarded,
trembling with fear.

I was the prowler, breaking and entering,
leaving the scene, lost in the guilt
of accusing, colluding, expunging a life.
I was that woman, aide and abettor,
letter of the law.

Sarasota Sunrise

Condo monoliths gleam white in early sunlight,
rimming the Bay's crescent in a wide grin;

lime-green signs suspended above an empty highway
point the way to the beach, gated suburb, shopping mall.

We look down on the roof of La Dolce Vita
from the fifteenth floor, watch shiny Matchbox cars

scuttle into parking slots, early risers trickle
into the internet café for a wake-up cup and the *Times*.

At Palm and Second, a man wheels his shopping cart,
takes up his post in a patch of sun against

the Bank of America, spits into his coffee cup,
sets his face into the scowl he'll wear all day,

muttering to himself, glaring at dog-walkers,
visitors who avert their eyes.

After the sun fades, he shuffles
to the Dumpster behind the post office,

parks his cart, tamps the gravel smooth.
Removing his tired face, he folds it

under his head and lies down to wait,
slack-jawed, for another sunrise.

La Doncella

Photo: In "Argentina, Museum Unveils Inca Maiden Frozen 500
    Years": *New York Times*, 9/11/07

Why are you smiling, Doncella?

Was it your mother who carried you
to the mountaintop altar made of ice,
kissed you, brushed away bits of coco leaves
still clinging to your upper lip,
folded your arms across your lap
until sleep dropped its frozen chin
on your chest? Was it she who placed
a clay doll beside you as you slept?

Who wove your shirt,
now stiff with frost, who adorned it
with loops and beads, fastened
a necklace of bone around your neck?
Who tenderly braided your hair into ropes
and then abandoned you?

Crowds of tourists visit
the Museum of High Altitude
to gape inside the acrylic cylinder,
push the button to illuminate your figure,
glistening with a crystal sheen fit for a goddess.
They give you immortality, lost child,
as if you chose it.

Nine-thirteen 2001: Going Home

Two days later
at Penn Station
the crowd pushes
down the escalator
rigid bodies
funnel into passenger cars
stream backward
past windows
inflamed eyes peering ahead
not daring to look out
Slack-jawed we sit
on baggage in aisles
blocking exits
cough out our stories
cascades of asbestos
pillows of ash dropping
in unearthly layers
voices muffled
eyes raked with grit
We find connections
murmured phrases
a wife lost then found
a meeting canceled
a friend weeping
into his cell phone
on the fourteenth floor
Images fall like angels

tumors nestle into lungs
as the train leans around curves
its wails parting plumes of wheat
bent in bereavement
the force of its trajectory
dispersing trails
of rubble and crushed paper
on the track
Torsos in woolen coats
sway side to side
nine hours to reach a station
out of danger
grown unfamiliar
changed beyond knowing
where leaf-strewn streets are empty
except for the smell
of burning.

September 2005

The papery gray nest hangs
like an overgrown melon from the shed,
yellow jackets diving, sniping,
flying in disoriented circles,
as the meshed man from Pest-Away
leaves hills of dead bees
scattered across the pavement,
removing all but a poisoned fragment,
which, he explains, will prevent stragglers
from re-nesting under a nearby eave.

Today the headline announces
that those remaining in New Orleans
after Katrina will be *forcibly evacuated,*
resistors and looters arrested, and stragglers
frantic on rooftops in the Ninth Ward,
swarming down the river of Ste. Claude St.,
camped like slaves on wrought-iron balconies,
will be resettled in the Astrodome,
or shipped to Utah. On TV,

Hardy Jackson points to the rubble
where his house once stood,
tells how he waited for rescue hanging
from a tree branch, how he grabbed
for his wife's hand as she sank,
how he searched the storm's jetsam
for his kids and grandkids for three days.
I'm lost, he says. *Just lost.*

3
...calling out one name

This Old House: A Photograph

My cousin texted me a photo of my old house,
looking a lot smaller than I remember,

painted Williamsburg Red with ivory trim,
not the all-white center entrance of my childhood.

Neat hedges replace unruly forsythias
on each side of the pillared porch;

gone are the sparse grassy patches beneath tall maples,
whose ancient roots once lifted the sidewalk,

all swapped for ornamental saplings and new cement,
velvety lawns edged with perennials.

Silent now, the wind-slap of wet laundry
as it hangs on the backyard clothesline,

the click of high heels down Vassar Street
on the way to the bus stop or corner grocery.

No more cries of Red Rover or Alley-Infree
on summer afternoons,

or Czerny and major triads
stumbling through the bay window.

Now, only the dry sputter of a motorcycle
or electric trimmer moves the air;

this neighborhood is sedate, urbane,
peopled by millennials, whose kids

bus daily to charter academies, and leave
for summer camp right after the final school day.

Yet I can still hear the grammar-school bell clanging—
arrival, lunchtime, dismissal—

steadily measuring the breadth of my days,
as fat pigeons mumble in the neighbor's gutter

and bees celebrate their good fortune
among bunches of lilacs dripping perfume.

The Brown Chevy

Sunday was the only day my father
didn't drive to Canandaigua, leaving at 7,
50 miles each way over rutted roads,

to open the store, check on the boy
he'd hired to sweep, carry cartons
of new merchandise to the basement for sorting,

re-stock the shelves with girdles and sweaters,
the racks with woolen skirts on hangers,
returning in the dark, long after supper.

Summer Sundays I watched splotches of sweat
grow on his tee-shirt as he mowed the lawn,
re-seeded bare spots under the maples,

strung a clothesline fence
around the edges to keep dogs away,
swept spinners from the front porch,

while the brown Chevy stood idle in the driveway,
simmering with heat, reeking of Camels,
waiting to ignite, or so it seemed to me.

But some Sundays, after the sprinkler, piano practice
and kitchen sink went silent, he'd appear on the porch
and boom out, "Come on, kiddos."

We'd pile in the Chevy, mother in crisp cotton,
my sister and I scrunching our skirts in our hands,
to pull open door-handles too hot to touch.

Daddy lit up, gave it the gas, drummed the wheel
with tobacco-stained fingers, while we stuck our heads out,
wind-slapped, gasping, cruising past the city limits

to Irondequoit where he'd point out cornfields,
spotted cows, sleek horses grazing,
as if he were a tour-guide in a foreign country.

At the top of a dirt road,
we'd spy the dairy at Idlebrook Farms
shimmering like a white castle, no brook in sight.

We waited in line, knowing the white-hatted scooper
would never run out of chocolate almond fudge.
"How 'bout this ice cream, Rue?" he'd say to mother

who'd nod and gather napkins
as we licked the sides of cones, dripping
on soon-to-be-laundered blouses.

On the sticky ride home, buzzing with sugar,
my sister and I slouched in the backseat,
sun low in the sky, while my father

whistled quietly—"Lady of Spain"—
driving the brown Chevy
clear into next week

home in time to re-start the sprinklers,
set the table for supper,
catch Jack Benny at 7.

Multitudes

So many stars. So many babies dreaming in their cribs.
So many stars dreaming of being the one American Idol.
So many in the audience, wearing so many tattoos, jeans,
studded jackets, so many purple hairs bristling
from so many scalps, so many bald heads shining.

Millions of early risers drinking so many cups of coffee,
racing to driveways, revving up motors, speeding past
masses of poplars along the road, medians glowing with
profusions of daffodils, cosmos in endless borders,
converging at countless intersections, where parades

of feet cross between the lines, hurrying through labyrinths
of trash to get to the shopping mall or the office or to
school, where cafeterias teem with children sitting at long
tables, eating so many ham and cheese sandwiches,
each one daydreaming of that time at Rehoboth or Sanibel

or Coney Island, of getting lost in a sea of beach towels,
a tsunami of tears, an infinite blur of sand and squawk,
searching to find among the multitudes,

a single sunburned face,
star-spangled bathing suit,
Ray Bans pushed back
over a red bandana,
cherry-tipped fingers
shading sun-struck eyes,
a voice tremulous with fear,
calling out one name.

Recital
For Patty

My sister and I wait in the wings
to play the piano, center stage,
its black spine arched,
our grinning, gap-toothed adversary.

We clutch our handkerchiefs,
beseech our personal gods for stamina
and enough memory in our joints to carry us
steadily through the obstacle course
of arpeggios and counterpoint.

Daily Czerny fills our after-school,
moist summers at the piano,
Bach Inventions mingle
with sing-songs of jump rope,
the ringing of cicadas in the maples.

We walk a path precisely drawn for us,
sure-footed in conformity,
my fair-haired, gifted sister and I,
her dark disciple, eight years behind,

who mimics the arch of her hand,
every angle of the wrist, nod of the head,
who adores the poetry of her phrase,
remembers every note
of music she has played.

Now fifty years have passed—
my sister enters left, adjusts the bench and plays.
Whatever Schubert asks, she answers;
waiting in the wings, I understand.

Hallowéd Be Thy Name

During the first week at YWCA Camp Ononda
the girls picked last for every team
chose Chorus for our 6th hour activity,
united by an aversion to canoeing
and swimming in the icy lake,
and an abject terror of dodge-ball.

Each day we bounded from Crafts Cabin
to Assembly Hall for practice, perched on the edge
of the stage, bare legs swinging in glorious unison.
Cheered on by Beth, the music counselor,
we sang our hearts out, players on an elite team,
the loudest voices around the campfire.

We all knew the words to the familiar songs:
"Zip-a-Dee-Doo-Dah," "Make New Friends" in a round.
But when "The Lord's Prayer" was picked,
I was the only wordless camper.
"Don't you go to church?" they quizzed me.
"Don't you ask Jesus to forgive your trespasses?"

I didn't know the meaning of *trespasses*,
nor the strange 3-syllable word *hallowéd*.
My voice began to falter from the back row.
And when Visitors' Day finally came,
I waited for my parents alone and silent
at the edge of the road.

Family Portrait

Ben and Charlie sit on the front porch, coloring.
Grains of salt cling to their eyebrows, the golden
fuzz on their cheeks, whiten their fingers. Ben
has swapped his bathing suit for dry clothes,
borrowed from his older cousin, almost seven,
loves their bagginess, soft familiarity, the warmth
of Charlie's freckled arm next to his. He inhales
the sea-smell sharp in the late sun, catches the
even breathing of the waves and the far-off flap
of herons' wings pulling gently across the island
toward dusk. He lifts his crayon from the paper
and turns to Charlie. "I'm so happy, I'm sad," he says.

Parental Guidance

Peter holds his finger to the light
to show his son its full deformity,
the last digit on his left hand
still bent at the first knuckle

as it was thirty years ago
when they removed the pin that fastened the tip.
The finger, slim and agile then,
healed quickly, hooked easily

around the trumpet ring, the guitar frets,
pressed itself into the softness
of the catcher's mitt, and curled
into the palm so a pencil could glide free.

Ben listens as his father tells him
about his grandfather's garage,
the lure of the workbench
smelling of sawdust and varnish,

and the whir of the gleaming table saw.
He scarcely hears the warnings
about the dangers of power tools,
the consequences of unbridled curiosity.

With serious eyes, Ben examines
the tilted extremity, now thick and callused,
caresses its familiar shape, remembering
what Peter has forgotten:

the honor of scars,
the thrill of a shared story,
the power of a father's crooked finger
inside a small hand.

Ode to Jane

How could I imagine
at Spring's unfurling,
that such a being stirred inside
the envelope of my seed,
that my blood was rich enough,
my cord pliant enough
to deliver a separate spirit
nourished at my roots,
shaded in my shadow,
watered by my tears.

How could I conceive you,
gentle Jane?
And by what miracle
did that curled leaf of girl
become a woman generous and strong,
narrow-hipped and long-limbed,
with a face perpetually lit
by some internal florescence?

Daughter, who clutched my hand
even when I stumbled,
you touch it now to raise me when I fall,
warm the winters of my life
with your summer breath.

Holding On

Washed and spun through countless cycles,
Elmo's plush, his vivid red,

the smell of talc and milky breath, all lost;
fallen from the shelf, tossed in the trash.

Now gangly grandkids sprawl
in bed until noon. No need

for fingering a toy to sleep,
a fuzzy head tucked beneath a chin.

Suddenly, a vast sadness,
remembering how we once held

each other's bodies through the night,
curving knees under buttocks, bellies

fitting into hollows, recalling the cling
of arms, lips tracing cheeks, the smell

of hair and sex, the way our faces colored
when we woke, excited to drink our coffee,

step boldly through another day.
How safe we felt, how soft.

White Satin Shoes

(For Molly, in memoriam)

I found the perfect shoes for her wedding,
white satin platform pumps,

pleated rosebuds strung across the instep,
a little bigger than her normal size,

but just right to accommodate
the swelling of pregnancy.

Perfect, the bride told me, tears gathering.
Even in morning sickness, she'd designed

and stitched her own satin dress, lace veil,
taught her friend to weave tiny pearls

into the intricate braids
of her strawberry blonde hair.

That sun-blown June afternoon,
she stepped lightly at her father's elbow,

smiled side to side,
opened her arms wide to meet her groom

under a white crocheted chuppah,
three hearts racing.

She danced every dance at the reception
even when the shoes pinched,

slipping them off after
a careless guest spilled wine on them.

Weeks after the baby girl's heart stopped pumping
and the infant was named and borne away,

she found the shoes in the back of a closet,
satin stained, rosebuds come loose.

She placed them in a box
and buried them under a Mollybush,

where every June a veil of white bells rises,
covering the lush purple foliage with lace.

ᦸᡲᡠ

Home Destroyed by Fire. Eight Engines Respond. Family Displaced.
The Daily Freeman, 12/20/13

1. Fire Report

A farmhouse surrounded by woods,
wide porches cluttered with pots
of newly planted cuttings from the garden,
the screened back porch, piled
with art projects, Lego architecture.
Inside, an unfinished puzzle on the table,
husband and wife, two young boys
gathered before a new wood stove.

Cold cinders collected,
carried to the backyard,
dumped in the snow.
Sleep.

He wakes up choking,
kitchen in flames.
Screaming to his wife,
he races to the boys' bedroom,
wrenches them, still asleep, from their beds,
carries them complaining and heavy
into the frigid air,
into the dark unfriendly air.

They huddle in their underwear,
the smoke alarm shrieking,
fire engines wailing toward them,
too late to make a difference.
Embers rise, coughing black smoke
against the night sky, obliterating stars.

The four of them weep as their house,

their rollicking, singing house,
art-filled, learning-filled, fun-filled house,
story-filled, sweet-smelling house,
the mac-and-cheese-Thanksgiving turkey-
local-organic overflowing kitchen,
the office of creative work, of word-craft,
ideas on a clothesline, the studio of artworks,
oils and pastels, the glow-in-the dark stars,
ceramic handprints, Crayola landscapes,
the house of plans, of plants,
house of ardor, house of connection

burns to the ground.

2. Sweet Air

After the flashbacks fade,
they toe the acrid ashes looking for the lost,
resurrect singed photos, a walnut plank,
a guitar wrapped for Christmas.
Outside a jagged windowpane,
a flame of cardinal streaks above the rubble,
comes to rest on a snowbank.

They move together into the sweet air.
The Catskills bump the sky behind them.
The ice-edged Hudson rushes by.
Snow-covered evergreens, bare oaks fringe the lakes.
Frogs break the silence along the rail-trail.
This is not a new world.

Condo Living

What a mistake, to let the window-cleaners
remove the nest, sending our sparrows
in search of accommodations more fitting
than the open dryer vent outside my 7th floor window.

Vanished, the shadow fluttering across the patch
of morning sun on the Formica counter, the flap
of unidentified wings on the gray cement ledge.
Silent, the noisy squabbles over delectable morsels,
the vying for family rank and parental attention.

Nothing's left of the natural world
to squeeze under the sash
into these five cramped rooms,
no stray leaves stuck under door-jambs,
or garden soil tracked across carpets,
no squirrels hiding acorns up here.

Oh, how foolish to silence the swoosh
of dusty wings against the screen, erase
all trace of bone, abandoned feathers from the sill.
How sad to lose sight of those tight brown bodies
warming themselves in intricate aeries
at the edge of every opening,
no matter how incongruous, how unsuitable.

4

...where it still resounds

❧

Slip Knots

If only we could hold the daylight,
catch it before it burns mauve to ash
sliding behind the dunes, before
the sputter, the dusky calm
signal the day's departure.

Held in place by the heft of sheer brilliance,
the day shades its eyes at last,
knots slipping by design into evening,
loose ends tugged free by invisible winds
to drift over waves, braids unraveling,
letting go but keeping the curves
that shaped their fastening.

Even in shadow, we strain to grasp
the lingering strands of light—
a streak of moon, a heron's wing,
pulling us through the blindered night—
that we may bind each morning to the next.

Attraction

Scientists can easily explain
Why electrons spin around the atom,
Why stars embrace their suns, and waves the shore,
Why day draws night and night succumbs to dawn.
There is a complex chemistry at work
In bees' attraction to the ripening fruit,
The moth to the lamp, the tortoise to the dunes.

But on moonless nights, what guides
A mother's lips to find the fontanel?
And the dying—what urges them
To lift their faces toward the window, clinging
To a passing scrap of summer, glimpse of garden,
Each fragrant rose seducing them to enter
One more time its velvet orbit?

One Red Leaf

A spark has lodged in the hedge, tucked into the dense textile
of a euonymus bush, bright as a painted fingernail loosen-
ing a dark green ribbon, lush foliage suffering a single
ember intent on arson, but held suspended on the
season's cusp by moist heat and a bee's rasp,
until the day's shrinkage, its lowered light
and mellowed hum, nudge incendiary
September toward autumn's wick,
to roar into flames, ignite the
salvage edges of all grow-
ing things, spread its rash
scarlet in a contagion
of smoke, a crackle
of dry leaves, re-
leasing its acrid
breath and an
explosion of
crows into
the crisp
air.

Found Objects

I found your sailing hat in a drawer,
gray hair stuck in the band
where it grazed your neck.
Squinting, you check the wind
and turn the wheel to fill the sail.

I found your watch glinting
sunlight on the nightstand
your tanned wrist, broad-knuckled
hand on tiller, sander, rake,
on my arm, my lap.

A razor rests
on a bathroom shelf.
Smiling through the steam,
you stroke your cheeks,
satisfied at their smoothness.

Plans found on your workbench,
neatly measured, drawn and folded—
you show me the angle of the legs,
guiding my hand over the grain
when I bring lunch.

I took your camera to the glacier
and found your shadow,
brilliant blue, through the lens.

How could I think these objects
might contain your presence,
when I alone am keeper
of your longing to remain?

Envy

I listen
through a bedroom window—
whistle of my neighbor's kettle,
rattle of cup, of spoon on saucer.
Pale-fingered, trembling slightly,
she sets his morning tea before him.

He sips,
steam rising to fog his glasses,
takes them off to wipe them
on the flannel of his robe,
touches her arm gently—
tender praise.

A piece of toast,
perhaps some jam or honey,
faded china
on a flowered place mat,
quilted pot embracing
and embraced;
blinds half-raised
spill sunlight on the moment,
brimming over.

And I am
scalded by the beauty.

Souvenir

The carved wooden bell—
pendulous tongue,
flared lips,
scrolls etched
by a farmer's hand—
dangling from a peg
at the market
in Luang Prabang,
then from a hook outside
the front door
of the lake house,
where it hung

under fifteen snowfalls,
fifteen July suns,
announcing guests,
opening doors
until it cracked,
its sonorous clang
dulled to a clack,
kept there
as a reminder—

how once it summoned me,
two years widowed,
through the maze of tents,
over the din of artisans, hawkers,
past the incense of cumin,

fat-sizzled bits of lamb,
how its voice seduced me
down sinuous rows
until I saw it suspended,

turned it over,
warm in my palms,
chose it over a dozen
mute contenders,
and in that instant,
unlocked my grieving heart
to let you in.

Hair Kiss

An acquaintance tells me
she used to watch the flowering
of our romance, how you and I
held hands as we walked,
looked into each other's faces
when we spoke, how we connected
across a crowd of party-goers,
or at a table in a noisy restaurant.
What she remembers most
was the way we sat at concerts,
how we touched arms, and once
she noticed you turn and kiss my hair.
She was moved by this gesture.
I feel my eyes fill, recalling
after all this time exactly where I was,
and how that silent kiss on my hair
caressed my scalp, my neck, how it
traveled down my spine and entered
the deep space of happiness
where it still resounds.

Omen

I saw the signs, early on—
a bird slamming against the window,
an immense flock of ravens
circling our house, darkness
dropping from their wings.

I should have been prepared
for this vacancy. Ravenous,
it chases me room to room,
hiding behind cookbooks,
in empty drawers, burnt-out light bulbs,

follows me into the grocery store,
accompanies me to dinner parties,
lodges in my voice, hoarse from disuse,
sleeps in my bed under cover,
among a pile of pillows.

The mirror's image dissolves in steam,
my footsteps muffle along a vanishing path.
Now the elms outside my window
raise their pale palms in surrender.
Nothing left to hold before the winter.

Making Plans

We plan, god laughs. (Yiddish Proverb)

Why sing praise for one more day?

With every second of tomorrow
accounted for, we circle days
on the calendar as if we owned them,
buy plane tickets and sunscreen,
envision weddings and births,
the small triumphs of the soul.

We plead and wheedle,
bargaining for more time,
take another step every day
along the path to somewhere,
while this antic god,
who delights in a good joke,

accepts our gratitude
amused by our foolishness,
giving us Mozart and a sky-full of stars—
then without warning
snatches them with a flourish
from our outstretched hands.

We Never Went to Bear Lake

The signs are still there, pointing the way
to a destination we could only imagine.
When we'd approach the turn-off
on the way to our summer house, we'd say,
"Let's go to Bear Lake—well, maybe next time,"

winking and laughing,
knowing we'd ignore the arrows,
secretly planning to avoid
the Bear Lake Campgrounds at all costs
whenever we passed the intersection.

We weren't a bit inclined
to see hidden blue water, or hear
the swish of a large furry mother
leading her cubs to sniff at our campfire,
not even tempted to glimpse a spangled sky
or the flicker of mating fireflies
through the flap of a tent.

Our future depended upon postponement.
"Leave something for next time," we said.

Never-Ending

You urged me to throw away
the orchid plant we'd nurtured for three years.
"Be grateful," you said, "for two years
of lavish blooms, velvety yellow, blush centers,
exotic stems arcing toward the light."
It was the third year that grieved us,
blossoms smaller, dropping off one by one,
no replacements in sight despite our efforts.
"No," you said, "it's over."

After you died, I ignored the pot on a low shelf
until a thin green shoot reached the window.
I felt you guide me to lift it toward the light, saying
"water and watch," grateful when it bore buds,
first one, then multitudes, delivering
overlapping blossoms—I counted fifty-three—
all shining for me in sunlight
and after dark, a profusion of stars.

Angkor: Frieze at Bayon Temple

A kneeling woman rests her forehead on a stone
and weeps to learn her husband has been eaten by a tiger.
On either side, two messengers reach out,
hands cupped to catch her tears.

Above them, gods and demons swirl and struggle,
spill to jungles dense with elephants and monkeys,
churning oceans overflow in waves of mortal combat,
spiral down to peasants living out their days
unmindful of the tumult overhead.

It's not edifice that steals my breath,
but architect, whose spirit soared to reach
beyond the rock. Not frieze, but sculptor,
who saw pathos in each myth, each human life,

the weeping widow, coldness of the stone,
her drooping shoulders, curving spine,
her loosened hair, the healing hands
that soothe her crumbling heart.

Adagio Assai

Driving home from the shopping mall
where I returned the pajamas
I bought him before he died,

I heard the Ravel piano concerto
on public radio—the jazzy first movement,
and then, oh, the slow one,

the piano's voice a sigh,
unbearably separate,
pure loneliness falling

like the last November leaf,
or the notes of a single winter bird
dropping from an unseen branch,

each phrase so filled with longing
I had to pull over, weeping for my lost life,
no one left to tell.

That evening, waiting alone in an empty row
for a concert to begin, I turned
to see my friend Kathy slide in beside me.

"I heard the Ravel Concerto
on the car radio today," she said.
"The solo piano in the Adagio—

so solitary, so forlorn,
I pulled over to listen,
tried to call you, but you weren't home."

The Girlfriends

When the husbands have disappeared,
the children moved away,
when mornings become a slow routine,
and evenings slog through endless reruns,
the girlfriends appear.

They understand the pall of loose ends.
Wired for telepathy, they feel the message
shaking them from sleep, interrupting
their own daily rituals, urging them to
tap your name on their Contacts list,

make dates for dinner before the concert,
sip martinis together at neighborhood cafés,
discuss the Middle East, a recent poem
or condo gossip, the grandkids,
a good movie or a bad hip.

They take turns driving to the colonoscopy,
not knowing what will turn up, but ready
with a flower and some chicken soup.
What happens when they, or you,
are picked off by some cancer or stroke

of fate? Who will be left to give advice,
or take it? Who will critique
the new haircut, weep with you
at the opera or on the front porch?
Where will we turn next to find true love?

Earphones

Here I am,
plugged into my iPhone,
cleaning drawers and closets
while Rubenstein on the Cloud
plays Chopin Nocturnes,
one after another.
I throw out your old credit cards
and prescriptions,
your driver's license
and scribbled passwords,
coming across your rimless glasses,
which I should donate
to poorly sighted people
but can't let go,
seeing them so clearly on your face
as you turn and lift your head in the mirror.

Who can say the dead never return,
when here is Arthur Rubenstein,
erect at the Steinway,
fluff of white hair undisturbed
even as he tackles
the most difficult arpeggios,
his fingers singing each haunting melody
by Frederic Chopin, dark-eyed and gaunt,

who is here, weeping
through a tiny wire into my ear
for his lost love, his lost homeland,
his sighs keening across the keyboard?

And here you are,
your spectacled face
with me all day.

You Were My Cup

You were my cup, I was your nectar.
You were my blanket, I was your heat.
You were my ladle, I was your nourishment.
You were my scripture, I was your ink.

You were my shoulders, I was your bones,
You were my ears, I was your song.
You were my lungs, you were my heart,
Mine for the breathing, mine for the bleeding.

You were the trunk, the limbs, the sap.
I was the shade, the leaf in the wind.
You were the yellow-bird who lit me,
I was the nest you settled on.

You were the poem, the voice, the choir,
You were the candle in the night,
You were the gold of the morning sun,
You were my wine. I am your cup.

Breath: A Blessing

May you keep safe within you
the breath god blows into your nostrils,
inhale the scents of lilac, ocean brine,
sun-baked sand and mossy ponds rippling with life,
harbor the wind that chafes your cheeks,
let the lure of musk and honey, the sharpness of sweat,
the hearth's sweet vapors on misty mornings
rush into every crevice of your body.

May the cacophony of geese returning
lift your eyes, and the gentle peck of rain on pine
fill the mute places of your heart.
Draw the plum's tartness, the chili's sting
through your parched lips, let the light of the sun
pour into your eyes until they overflow,
and your lungs fill with air so rich and heady,
you will need nothing else.

May you leap up shining with gratitude
and breathe the peace of Shechinah's presence.
Then from the feathery space
between the wings of cherubim,
you will hear an exhalation so beautiful
the thrush in the aspen will stop mid-song to listen,
and thunder will curl docile into its cloud,
stunned by the sound of god's name.

Photo by Linda Gellman

BORN in Rochester, NY, **Susan Dworski Nusbaum** received her BA from Smith College and her law degree from the University of Buffalo Law School. She lives in Buffalo, N.Y., where she has worked as a teacher, arts administrator, and most recently as a criminal prosecutor. She has been a frequent participant in the Chautauqua Institution Writers' Festival and Chautauqua Writers' Center poetry workshops, and has served on the Board of the Chautauqua Literary Arts Friends.

Her work has appeared in numerous publications, including *The Connecticut Review*, *Poetry East*, *Nimrod International Journal*, *Chautauqua Literary Journal*, *Chautauqua*, *Harpur Palate*, *Wisconsin Review*, *The Sow's Ear*, *Earth's Daughters*, *Artvoice*, and *The Buffalo News*. Her book, *What We Take With Us*, was published by Coffeetown Press in 2014.

You can find Susan online at:

www.susandworskinusbaum.com.

33028877R00085